CORNERSTONES OF FREEDOM™

THE BOSTON MASSACRE

BY PETER BENOIT

CHILDREN'S PRESS®
An Imprint of Scholastic Inc.
New York   Toronto   London   Auckland   Sydney
Mexico City   New Delhi   Hong Kong
Danbury, Connecticut

BRINGING HISTORY to LIFE

Content Consultant
James Marten, PhD
Professor and Chair, History Department
Marquette University
Milwaukee, Wisconsin

Library of Congress Cataloging-in-Publication Data

Benoit, Peter, 1955–
  The Boston Massacre / by Peter Benoit.
  pages cm.—(Cornerstones of freedom)
  Includes bibliographical references and index.
  ISBN 978-0-531-28201-4 (lib. bdg.) — ISBN 978-0-531-27666-2 (pbk.)
  1. Boston Massacre, 1770—Juvenile literature. I. Title.
  E215.4.B46 2013
  973.3'113—dc23   2013000075

All rights reserved. Published in 2014 by Children's Press, an imprint of
Scholastic Inc.
Printed in the United States of America 113

1 2 3 4 5 6 7 8 9 10 R 23 22 21 20 19 18 17 16 15 14

Photographs © 2014: AP Images/North Wind Picture Archives: cover,
3, 4, 5 bottom, 11, 23, 32, 33, 34, 47, 48; Architect of the Capitol: 54, 55;
Bridgeman Art Library: 7 (Brooklyn Museum of Art, New York, USA/
Carll H. de Silver Fund), 20 (Private Collection), 51 (Museum of Fine Arts,
Boston, Massachusetts, USA/Gift of Miss Grace W. Treadwell), 30, 56
top (Massachusetts Historical Society, Boston, MA, USA), 50, 59 (Private
Collection/Courtesy of Swann Auction Galleries); Corbis Images: 18, 37,
56 bottom; Getty Images: back cover, 36 (Fotosearch), 29 (MPI); Internet
Archive/Library of the Public Archives of Canada: 41; iStockphoto/Steven
Wynn: 13; Library of Congress: 38, 45, 46, 58; The Art Archive/Picture
Desk/Culver Pictures: 6; The Granger Collection: 5 top, 8, 12, 17, 28, 39, 49;
The Image Works: 16 (Print Collector/HIP), 4 top, 4 bottom, 10, 14, 15, 19,
22, 25, 26, 27, 35, 42, 44, 57.

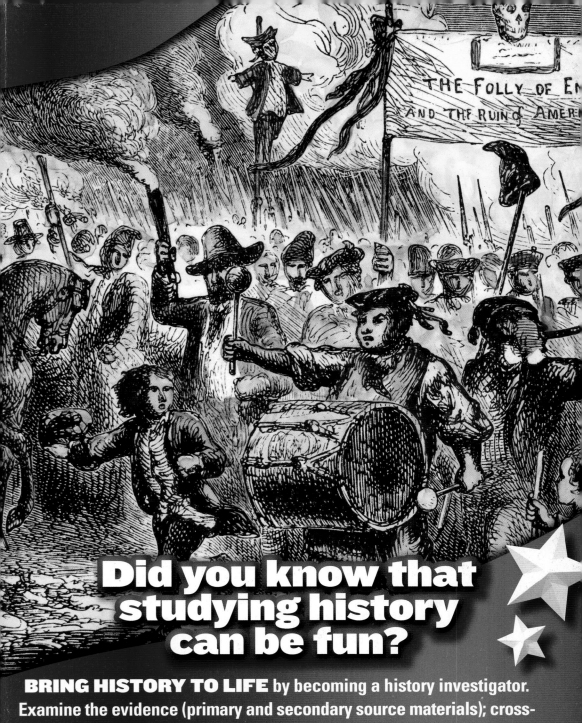

THE FOLLY OF E[ng...]
AND THE RUIN[f] AMER[...]

Did you know that studying history can be fun?

BRING HISTORY TO LIFE by becoming a history investigator. Examine the evidence (primary and secondary source materials); cross-examine the people and witnesses. Take a look at what was happening at the time—but be careful! What happened years ago might suddenly become incredibly interesting and change the way you think!

Contents

Taxing the Colonies

With the help of Native American allies, England defeated France in the French and Indian War.

In 1763, Great Britain won the French and Indian War in North America. As a result, it gained complete control of what is now the eastern United States. However, the war also left Britain saddled with crushing debt. Members of **Parliament** reasoned that because Britain had secured the American **frontier**, it would be fair to raise new taxes on its North American **colonies**.

The new taxes faced opposition in Parliament and the colonies. British officer Isaac Barré pointed out that Britain would never have secured the frontier without the sacrifices of American colonists. Boston's Benjamin Franklin echoed Barré's argument in 1766, but such complaints did not keep Parliament from creating more new taxes and sending more troops to the colonies.

Parliament's actions made many colonists angry and distrustful. Despite this, most colonists still thought of themselves as British citizens. They hoped to convince Parliament that its governing of the colonies was unfair.

In 1765, Isaac Barré delivered his famous "Sons of Liberty" speech, which argued against Great Britain's increased taxation of the North American colonies.

LASTED FROM 1754 TO 1763.

CHAPTER 1

POWDER KEG

A celebratory fireworks display in London, England, marked the signing of the Treaty of Paris.

THE FRENCH AND INDIAN WAR

was ended with the 1763 Treaty of Paris, which called for massive land exchanges among France, Spain, and Great Britain. This transfer of land forever changed the balance of power in North America. Britain suddenly possessed a long stretch of wild frontier. Maintaining peace with Native Americans along this frontier required a large army. The cost of maintaining these military forces plus the cost of the war itself doubled Britain's national debt. To leaders in Parliament, taxing the colonies seemed a natural way to reduce the debt while maintaining a standing army in North America.

More than one-fourth of the total area of Boston, Massachusetts, is water, making it an ideal location for a port.

The American Revenue Act

Parliament wasted no time collecting these taxes. It put the American Revenue Act in place in April 1764. The Revenue Act named several goods that colonists could **export** only to Britain. One of these goods, lumber, was a major part of the **economy** in the New England colonies. Any merchant or ship's captain who failed to accurately report trade of these goods would be taken to court and fined heavily. Suspects were presumed guilty and were required to prove their innocence. Though this act affected relatively few people directly, it made the colonists aware that Parliament intended to tax them heavily. While Parliament had always had the power to tax the colonists, it had often failed to enforce such taxes in the past.

The Stamp Act

The following year, the debate over taxes sharpened because of the Stamp Act. The act required all American colonists to pay a tax on a wide variety of papers, such as licenses, legal documents, and newspapers. Even playing cards were taxed. The Stamp Act's effects were felt by rich and poor alike, and it met broad resistance. Colonists were angered most that Parliament had taxed them without first seeking the approval of colonial **legislatures**. The colonists themselves had no say in the act's creation. In protest, Virginia's legislature soon approved several new laws to limit the Stamp Act. Newspapers published reports of Virginia's resistance, inspiring other colonies to act. By the end of 1765, eight more colonies had issued laws against the Stamp Act.

Stamp Act protests sometimes became violent riots.

THE FOLLY OF ENGLAND AND THE RUIN OF AMERICA

A City Divided

In Massachusetts, resistance erupted in violence. The colony's leadership was already divided. Governor Francis Bernard was not widely trusted. When the office of chief justice had become available in 1760, Bernard had appointed Thomas Hutchinson. This angered supporters of the other candidate, James Otis Sr.

A tense situation became much worse when news of the hated Stamp Act arrived. Hutchinson's brother-in-law, Andrew Oliver, was appointed stamp distributor for the colony. A group of enraged men called the Loyal Nine met in Boston and plotted against Oliver and Hutchinson. The Loyal Nine eventually ransacked their homes and forced Oliver to resign his position. Their success encouraged many

Governor Francis Bernard was in charge of overseeing both Massachusetts and New Jersey.

other merchants, artisans, and professionals to join similar organizations. These groups were eventually unified as the Sons of Liberty, with Samuel Adams as their dynamic leader.

As a result of the colonists' protests, the Stamp Act was discontinued after one year. However, relief was short-lived. In 1767, Parliament began passing a new series of laws called the Townshend Acts. These laws taxed **imports** of glass, lead, paper, and tea. They were extremely unpopular. Boston

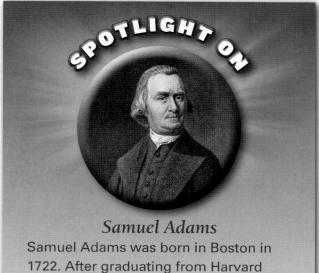

SPOTLIGHT ON

Samuel Adams

Samuel Adams was born in Boston in 1722. After graduating from Harvard College in 1740, he studied law and tried unsuccessfully to start several businesses. He then began working as a tax collector and started to participate in local politics.

Adams soon developed a reputation for his resistance to Parliament's taxation of the North American colonies. He spoke out against the 1764 Sugar Act, which placed a tax on molasses, and helped spur riots to protest the Stamp Act. In the summer of 1765, he founded the Sons of Liberty, a group that would play a major role in the colonies' struggle to free themselves from British rule.

threatened to erupt in violence. In February 1768, Adams issued a statement called the Massachusetts Circular Letter, which expressed the belief that only colonial legislatures should have the power to create new taxes in the colonies.

A FIRSTHAND LOOK AT
THE MASSACHUSETTS CIRCULAR LETTER

Samuel Adams's influential Massachusetts Circular Letter argued that the Townshend Acts were unfair because colonists had no representatives in Parliament. See page 60 for a link to read the text of the letter online.

Adams's letter won the support of the Massachusetts House of Representatives and was spread to other colonies. Wills Hill, Lord Hillsborough, a member of Parliament in charge of the colonies, demanded that the Massachusetts government officially stop supporting the letter. The colony's leaders refused. Caught in the middle between Lord Hillsborough and the Sons of Liberty, Governor Bernard dissolved the Massachusetts legislature. Bernard's

Wills Hill, Lord Hillsborough, was the secretary of state for the North American colonies from 1768 until 1772.

Customs officers were sometimes dragged from their homes and harassed by the Sons of Liberty.

action had far-reaching consequences. With no official way to make complaints against Parliament's actions, Boston's citizens turned increasingly to mob violence.

Mobs

The mobs attacked British officials and **boycotted** British goods in an attempt to pressure Parliament. Britain in turn cracked down on merchants who opposed the **customs** agents. However, threats of violence made it difficult for customs agents to enforce the law.

Customs agents and other government officials met with strong resistance from the colonists when they tried to enforce the laws handed down by Parliament.

In May 1768, the arrival of the HMS *Romney*, a 50-gun warship, once again shifted the balance of power in favor of customs officials. By June 10, customs inspectors were prepared to seize John Hancock's ship, *Liberty*. Hancock had long been a vocal critic of the customs service. A mob gathered to resist the seizure, but *Liberty* was eventually towed out to the *Romney*, which kept its guns trained on the crowd of protesters. A riot broke out, and customs agents were severely beaten. The mob soon grew to several thousand. The rioters surged through the streets, searching for customs agents to punish. Violence had become the standard reaction to British intrusions.

Alarmed by the breakdown of order on the streets of Boston and the attacks on customs officials, Britain sent its 14th and 29th **Regiments** to restore order and protect customs officials. Citizens were furious with Governor Bernard for agreeing to allow the troops into Boston. Two thousand British soldiers now watched over Boston's 16,000 citizens. The troops were temporarily housed in Faneuil Hall and the Old State House, where local government meetings were held. Many of Boston's citizens were convinced that the soldiers were placed there to disrupt the protest meetings held by local leaders who opposed Parliament.

Constructed in 1742, Faneuil Hall remains an important Boston landmark today.

Around 1770, Paul Revere created this engraving titled *A View of Part of the Town of Boston in New-England and Brittish Ships of War Landing their Troops! 1768.*

Boston Turns Bloody

An already dangerous situation was rapidly becoming worse. Paul Revere, a silversmith active in the Sons of Liberty, had produced an engraving of the landing of British troops. The engraving portrayed Adams's home city of Boston as a place of peace and order. In reality, the city was split by political rivalries and increasingly ruled by mobs.

The newly arrived British soldiers met with some success protecting customs agents. However, Samuel Adams urged a boycott of taxed British goods more strongly than ever. Adams forced people to go along with the boycott by publicly naming merchants who violated it. The Sons of Liberty punished anyone who dared to do business with a boycott violator. Adams also wrote a series of articles published in the *New York Journal* that spread news of the military occupation of Boston.

On February 22, 1770, a sign was placed outside the shop of boycott violator Theophilus Lillie. His neighbor Ebenezer Richardson tried to take the sign down. Richardson was already unpopular for playing a major role in John Hancock's ship being seized by customs officials. A crowd of boys turned their fury on Richardson as he tried to remove the sign from Lillie's shop. They pelted him with mud and rocks. Richardson responded by firing his gun into the crowd of boys, killing eleven-year-old Christopher Seider (sometimes spelled "Snider").

The shooting of Christopher Seider by Ebenezer Richardson during the British goods boycott shocked the people of Boston. Many of them wanted to see Richardson hanged. Seider's funeral was paid for by the city and attended by thousands of people. It was an emotional event that pushed hatred of British soldiers and customs officers to a dangerous new level. On the day of the funeral, the *Boston Gazette* lamented the boy's death. It also made note of Richardson's refusal to go along with the boycott and stated the hope that Seider's death would be a warning against more violence in the city.

CHAPTER 2

BOSTON ERUPTS

At meetings of the Sons of Liberty, angry colonists shouted in protest against their treatment by the British government.

EVEN BEFORE CHRISTOPHER
Seider's death, it was clear that the presence of
British soldiers in Massachusetts was a recipe for
disaster. The British military irritated Boston's
citizens. Confrontations between soldiers and
civilians had become a daily occurrence. Within a
week of Seider's death, the *Gazette* ceased reporting
skirmishes because they had become too numerous.
At this point, Boston's Sons of Liberty seized the
opportunity to protest against the British taxes.
Worse violence would soon erupt.

At ropewalks, long strands of material were laid out and then woven into ropes.

Fuel for the Fire

On Friday, March 2, 1770, at noon, Patrick Walker of Britain's 29th Regiment approached John Gray's rope-making business. Walker, like many other poorly paid troops, was looking for work. It was common for British soldiers to take side jobs in the colonies, and the practice had long irritated Boston's population. They were forced to compete for work against men they loathed. Gray's employee William Green asked Walker if he wanted work. Eager for the opportunity, Walker said yes. Green then hurled an insult at him. Walker stormed off, returning moments later with nine other soldiers, including Private William Warren, who would later play a role in the Boston Massacre. The rope makers drove them out using clubs. However, the soldiers soon returned, 40 strong and armed. Once again, the rope makers clubbed the soldiers and drove them away.

The next day, three soldiers fought with a trio of rope makers. Private John Rodgers of the 29th Regiment received a skull fracture. His commanding officer, Maurice Carr, wrote Thomas Hutchinson, who had recently become governor, concerning the conflicts with the rope makers. That evening, one of Carr's sergeants failed to answer roll call. The rumor spread that he had been murdered. On Sunday morning, Carr led an unauthorized search for the missing sergeant at John Gray's rope factory. Tensions had now reached the boiling point. All over Boston, people murmured that there would be a riot on Monday evening.

The British soldiers in Boston were constantly in conflict with the city's people.

On Monday morning, March 5, a notice was posted along Boston's streets. It stated that soldiers from the 14th and 29th Regiments would join forces to defend themselves against rioting citizens. The notice confirmed the rumors citizens had heard.

King Street, March 5

That night, bands of citizens and soldiers patrolled the cold, moonlit streets. A foot of icy snow lay on the ground and made walking difficult. Private Hugh White had been stationed at the corner of the Custom House on King Street. The three-story brick building contained all of Boston's customs records and collected revenue. Meanwhile, crowds of men and boys armed with shovels and swords assembled in front of Faneuil Hall. By now, the mob had swollen to nearly 300. It split into two loud and angry groups. One group headed up Cornhill to Murray's Barracks, the home of the 29th Regiment.

Soldiers were able to hold off the unruly mob pressing its way toward Murray's Barracks. Unable to break through the gates there, the crowd instead shouted insults and threw chunks of ice. They next turned their attention to the Custom House. White heard them approach. A man named Edward Garrick insulted Captain John Goldfinch of the 14th Regiment near the Custom House. Recognizing that Garrick meant to draw him into a fight, Goldfinch wisely chose to ignore him. Garrick persisted, enraging White. The sentry swung his gun, striking Garrick solidly on the

Private Hugh White was an 11-year veteran of the British army at the time of the Boston Massacre.

side of his head. Shortly, bells began to ring all over the city. Usually, they would signal fire, but not on this cold March night. Word spread quickly that the soldiers and citizens were fighting on King Street.

More citizens began moving toward the conflict. Seventeen-year-old Samuel Maverick headed to King Street after finishing a late dinner. Crispus Attucks hurried to the Custom House carrying a large cordwood stick. As the crowd grew larger, Hugh White became concerned for his safety. He backed up onto the steps of the Custom House, loaded his gun, and pointed it toward the crowd.

Violence erupted in the streets as the conflict between the soldiers and the colonists came to a head.

The mob responded by pressing in even closer, pinning White against the Custom House. By nine o'clock, Captain Thomas Preston ordered six privates and a corporal to rescue White. The angry mob closed in around these soldiers, trapping them with White. The soldiers stood together, forming a semicircle, with their backs to the Custom House.

Shots Fired

The crowd began to chant, "Kill them!" Some people threw snowballs and chunks of ice. Others, attempting to make the soldiers fight back, ran in front of them and hit their guns with wooden clubs. Merchant Richard Palmes stepped forward and warned Preston that his men must not fire. It was widely understood that soldiers could not use force against civilians without permission from civil authorities. However, a soldier could kill if his own life was in danger. Preston gave his word to Palmes that his men would not fire, though their guns were loaded. Then someone in the mob threw a club. It struck Private Hugh Montgomery.

Montgomery slipped on the ice and fell. Infuriated, he rose to his feet, pointed his musket toward the crowd, and fired. Then two more soldiers raised their guns and fired. Rope maker Samuel Gray spun around and crumpled on the street as he was struck in the

TODAY'S PERSPECTIVE

Crispus Attucks is often mentioned as being the first person who died in the Boston Massacre. However, that was only part of his legacy. In 1888, he and the other victims of the massacre were memorialized in a monument on Boston Common.

Attucks, who had an African American father and a Native American mother, had escaped from slavery as a child. In the 1850s, when many people were working to end slavery in the United States, he became a symbol of freedom. More than a century later, civil rights leader Martin Luther King Jr. spoke of Attucks in a speech on moral courage.

head. Two musket balls tore through the chest of Crispus Attucks. He collapsed, dying almost instantly.

YESTERDAY'S HEADLINES

A week after the Boston Massacre, the *Boston Gazette* published a graphic description of the dead and wounded at the bloody scene on King Street. The *Gazette* exposed a nerve among Boston's citizens. It claimed that British soldiers had "cruelly" interfered with efforts to rescue wounded civilians. Historians are divided on the accuracy of this article. Some believe it was an attempt to sway public opinion in advance of trials for the soldiers.

As the frenzied mob advanced, other soldiers fired. Sailor James Caldwell was also killed by a musket ball. Patrick Carr, crossing the street, felt a shot tear through his hip and strike his backbone. He lived for nine more days in agony. Young Samuel Maverick was killed when he was hit in the chest by a musket ball. Six others were badly injured, but remarkably they all survived.

Before a drop of blood had been shed, Governor Hutchinson had heard of lawless mobs roaming the streets. He hurried from his home to King Street, where he confronted Captain Preston. Hutchinson was too late. The damage was already done. He told Preston to take his troops back to the barracks before the violence grew any worse. Preston wisely agreed. Other soldiers

and *Crispus Attucks*, the unhappy victims who fell in the bloody Massacre of the Monday Evening preceeding !

On this Occasion most of the Shops in Town were shut, all the Bells were ordered to toll a solemn Peal, as were also those in the neighboring Towns of Charlestown Roxbury, &c. The Procession began to move between

A *Boston Gazette* obituary was illustrated with caskets bearing the names of the victims of the Boston Massacre.

of the 29th Regiment arrived to form a defensive shield around them. Hutchinson told the enraged citizens to go home, assuring them that justice would be done. As they trudged home, few could have imagined what shape that justice would take.

A FIRSTHAND LOOK AT

A BOSTON MASSACRE OBITUARY

A week after the Boston Massacre, the *Boston Gazette* published an obituary for the four people who died in the attack. Patrick Carr was not included, as he had not yet died from his wounds. The obituary includes an illustration of four black coffins and describes the funeral service held for the men. See page 60 for a link to see the entire obituary online.

CHAPTER 3

MANAGING THE CRISIS

Governor Hutchinson, shown here as a young man, acted quickly in the wake of the massacre.

HUTCHINSON IMMEDIATELY

met with judges John Tudor and Richard Dana, and Lieutenant Colonel William Dalrymple. As soldiers and civilians continued to scuffle outside, the four agreed that Preston and his men should be put on trial for their role in the massacre. Sheriff William Greenleaf promptly arrested Preston.

Samuel Adams (left) and the Sons of Liberty warned Governor Hutchinson (second from right) that more violence would follow the massacre if British troops were allowed to remain in Boston.

Meanwhile, a greater catastrophe had been narrowly avoided. On Monday night, riders sent to neighboring towns had alerted colonists of the trouble in Boston. Eager for revenge, thousands of armed men rode toward Boston, but they were turned back by British soldiers.

Public Outrage

Boston was still seething on Tuesday morning. Hutchinson called a council meeting at the Town House. Colonial officials pleaded with Hutchinson to order the soldiers to leave Boston. A Sons of Liberty committee composed of Samuel Adams, John Hancock, and others pressed the issue. They said more violence would follow unless troops were removed immediately. Dalrymple offered to remove the 29th Regiment, but the committee insisted the 14th be removed, too. Finally, after further discussion, Hutchinson and Dalrymple grudgingly agreed to remove both regiments. The 29th and 14th Regiments were ferried to Castle William, an island fort in the Boston Harbor.

Castle William was renamed Fort Independence after the Revolutionary War.

Against this backdrop, the city mourned. On Thursday, March 8, the caskets of Crispus Attucks, Samuel Gray, James Caldwell, and Samuel Maverick were carried along King Street during a funeral service. All the church bells of Boston tolled, and the city's shops were closed out of respect for the dead. The four caskets were laid to rest in a common grave alongside the body of Christopher Seider. When Patrick Carr died, he was buried with the others.

Pressing Charges

On Monday, March 12, the local government resolved to create a detailed account of the massacre. Over the next week, officers took sworn statements from 96 witnesses.

Today, visitors to Boston can view the common grave of Christopher Seider and the Boston Massacre victims.

The Remains of
SAMVEL GRAY
SAMVEL MAVERICK
JAMES CALDWELL
CRISPVS ATTVCKS
AND
PATRICK CARR

Victims of the Boston Massacre, March 5th, 1770, were here interred by order of the Town of Boston.

Here also lies buried the body of
CHRISTOPHER SNIDER

Aged 12 years, Killed February 22nd, 1770.

The innocent first victim of the struggles between the Colonists and the Crown, which resulted in INDEPENDENCE.

Placed by Boston Chapter S.A.R.
1906.

Some witnesses claimed to have seen gunfire coming from the Custom House, where British soldiers were stationed.

Joseph Warren, James Bowdoin, and Samuel Pemberton then prepared an official town report, titled *A Short Narrative of the Horrid Massacre in Boston*. The report traced the root of the crisis to the Stamp Act and the behavior of appointed customs officers.

The report placed ultimate responsibility for the actions of British troops on customs officers. Five of the 96 eyewitnesses claimed that they saw flashes of gunfire coming from the Custom House windows, indicating that customs officers directly participated in the massacre. There was some support for the claim. An **autopsy** of Crispus Attucks revealed that one of the musket balls that ripped through his chest came from a high angle. More than 6 feet (1.8 meters) tall, Attucks stood so high that none of the British soldiers could have fired on him from above.

This poem published on **March 5, 1772**, reflected the public outrage at Ebenezer Richardson's shooting of Christopher Seider.

Patrick Carr gave his remembrance of the massacre from his deathbed. He claimed that the mob had provoked the soldiers by hurling stones, ice, and clubs at them. In Carr's opinion, the soldiers on King Street had acted in self-defense. His testimony would play a major role when the eight soldiers came to trial.

While testimony was taken from eyewitnesses, the grand jury met. As expected, it **indicted** Ebenezer Richardson in the shooting of Christopher Seider. It also indicted Thomas Preston and the eight soldiers involved in the massacre. In a surprising move, the jury also indicted four civilians who had participated in the massacre. Although none of the high-ranking customs commissioners were indicted, all but one fled Boston to avoid the revenge of angry colonists.

Influencing the Public

Engraver Henry Pelham made a sketch of the massacre that distorted several key features. In Pelham's drawing, seven soldiers fire at the same time on unarmed citizens. Captain Preston stands behind them with his sword raised. The British soldiers stand in the middle of the street and the civilians have their backs to the wall, making the soldiers look like a firing squad. A wispy plume of smoke floats from a Custom House window.

Silversmith Paul Revere created an engraving based on Pelham's drawing. In Revere's engraving, a sign reading "Butcher's Hall" is added to the front of the Custom House

SPOTLIGHT ON

Paul Revere

Paul Revere was born in Boston's North End in 1735. A well-known silversmith by profession, he is today remembered for his patriotism. Though not one of the Loyal Nine, he was a major force in the Sons of Liberty.

Revere's engravings of major events helped influence public opinion. His engraving of British troops landing in Boston portrayed the city as a place of peace and strong morals. His engraving of the Boston Massacre showed British troops brutally murdering defenseless citizens and linked the red coats of British soldiers to the red of colonists' spilled blood.

Though inaccurate, Paul Revere's engraving of the massacre is still the best-known image of the incident.

and the plume of smoke has become a large cloud. Pelham was furious that Revere had altered his vision of the event. Revere's engraving appeared on the cover of the *Short Narrative* and was seen by many people, so that was the version generally accepted as true.

A FIRSTHAND LOOK AT
PAUL REVERE'S BOSTON MASSACRE ENGRAVING

Paul Revere's engraving took many liberties with the details of the massacre. However, it stuck in the public's mind and helped to spread the idea that British troops had murdered civilians in cold blood. See page 60 for a link to read more about Revere's engraving online.

However, other versions varied from the *Short Narrative*. In late spring 1770, a London author published a pamphlet drawn from the sworn testimony of British soldiers and Boston civilians. *A Fair Account of the Late Unhappy Disturbance at Boston in New England* was more balanced than the *Short Narrative*. Because it placed a share of the blame on Boston civilians, it renewed many of the harsh feelings that had slowly begun to ease.

Controversy

The *Fair Account* also contained Andrew Oliver's report on the Governor's Council meeting of March 6, the day after the massacre. The Sons of Liberty

The *Short Narrative* influenced many people's opinions of the massacre.

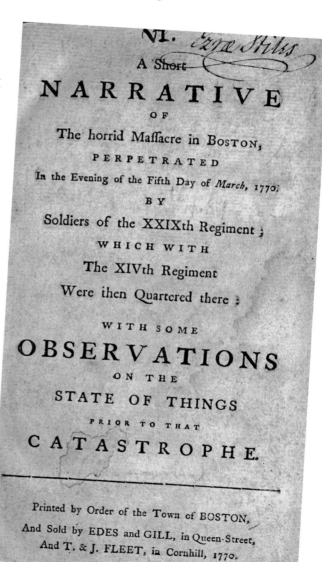

VI. *Ezra Stiles*

A Short

NARRATIVE

OF

The horrid Maſſacre in BOSTON,

PERPETRATED

In the Evening of the Fifth Day of *March*, 1770;

BY

Soldiers of the XXIXth Regiment;

WHICH WITH

The XIVth Regiment

Were then Quartered there;

WITH SOME

OBSERVATIONS

ON THE

STATE OF THINGS

PRIOR TO THAT

CATASTROPHE.

Printed by Order of the Town of BOSTON,

And Sold by EDES and GILL, in Queen-Street,

And T. & J. FLEET, in Cornhill, 1770.

A VIEW FROM ABROAD

The *Fair Account* pamphlet created controversy in Boston. The *Short Narrative* said the root of the massacre was the appointment of customs officers years earlier, while the *Fair Account* said it started with the confrontations between soldiers and rope makers. This amounted to a denial of the colonists' complaints.

While the *Short Narrative* referred to the March 5 event as a "horrid massacre," London newspapers referred to it by the more neutral "incident on King Street." These newspapers may not have considered an event in a remote colonial outpost of 16,000 inhabitants important, as London's population was rapidly approaching one million. It is more likely that the British government wanted to make this event seem unimportant, as it could damage Britain's relations with its other colonies.

distrusted Oliver. Samuel Adams was already familiar with Oliver, who had been appointed stamp distributor five years earlier. The Sons of Liberty had persuaded Oliver to not accept that appointment, by destroying his warehouse. Oliver now took advantage of his opportunity for revenge. He claimed that at a council meeting before March 5, councilor Royall Tyler had mentioned that a plot was in place to have soldiers and customs officers removed. Oliver went on to imply that councilors had forced him to alter their records to hide the plot.

The councilors were furious. Oliver had distorted the facts and betrayed their trust by releasing council records. The council appointed a committee of five to investigate Oliver's claims. All of the claims were swiftly shown to be false. The council pointed out that Oliver had broken their trust by sending details of its meetings to London. Oliver argued that it was his duty as an officer appointed by the king. Once again, all of Boston was on edge. There was no hope for a fair trial in such conditions. The city was now unified in opposition to Hutchinson and Oliver.

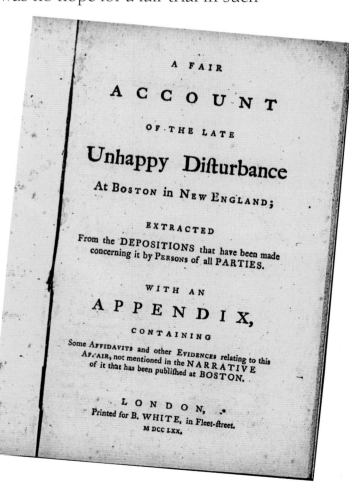

A FAIR

ACCOUNT

OF·THE LATE

Unhappy Difturbance

At BOSTON in NEW ENGLAND;

EXTRACTED

From the DEPOSITIONS that have been made concerning it by PERSONS of all PARTIES.

WITH AN

APPENDIX,

CONTAINING

Some AFFIDAVITS and other EVIDENCES relating to this AFFAIR, not mentioned in the NARRATIVE of it that has been publifhed at BOSTON.

LONDON,
Printed for B. WHITE, in Fleet-ftreet.
M DCC LXX.

The *Fair Account* contradicted the *Short Narrative* by arguing that the conflict between the soldiers and colonists began with the quarrel between the rope makers and the job-seeking troops.

CHAPTER 4

THE TRIALS

Future U.S. president John Adams agreed to serve as an attorney for the defense in the case against the British soldiers.

CAPTAIN PRESTON AND THE other soldiers involved in the massacre had been placed in jail in the early hours of March 6, after being allowed to state their side of the story. At that time, there couldn't have been any safer place in Boston for these men.

Immediately, Preston's friend James Forrest went in search of lawyers to represent him at the trial. Attorneys Josiah Quincy and Robert Auchmuty both refused to defend Preston unless Forrest could arrange for John Adams to join them. Remarkably, Adams agreed almost without hesitation. The three lawyers faced a major challenge. Four men were dead, another was mortally wounded, and six others were badly injured. There were many witnesses to these crimes. The attorneys began to build their defense, as resentment boiled in the streets of Boston.

Outraged over the massacre, the Sons of Liberty called for quick trials against Ebenezer Richardson and the soldiers who had participated in the shootings.

Searching for Justice

The trial could have begun by the end of March, but two of the four judges were ill. The trial was delayed. Judge Benjamin Lynde twice tried to resign rather than oversee the controversial trial. Governor Hutchinson refused both requests for him to act as judge for the trial.

With the Sons of Liberty pressing for justice, Ebenezer Richardson's trial was set for March 30. However, Richardson could find no lawyer willing to defend him. The court appointed Samuel Fitch to serve as his attorney. Fitch refused out of fear that defending such an unpopular client would make the public hate him. When the court repeated its demand, Fitch failed to show up for the new April 17 court date.

Josiah Quincy stepped in. On the day of the trial, angry men waited at the door with nooses. They were ready to hang Richardson. Inside the courtroom, a few others bent on revenge chanted, "Blood requires blood!" Quincy argued that Richardson had been under attack from a mob, but it was not enough to stop the jury from finding him guilty. Hutchinson worked to delay Richardson's execution, hoping to secure a royal **pardon**. Still thirsting for blood, the Sons of Liberty pressed for the trials of Preston and the other soldiers.

Facing the wrath of angry Bostonians, Josiah Quincy bravely agreed to defend Richardson at trial.

Captain Preston's trial began on October 24. Thanks to the arguments of Adams, Quincy, and Auchmuty, along with a lack of solid evidence, it took the jury only three hours to find him not guilty. Fearing that the people of Boston would attack him, Preston immediately fled to the safety of Castle William. Preston's **acquittal** hurt the chances of the other eight soldiers. With five people dead, someone had to be held accountable.

John Adams

Born in Massachusetts in 1735, John Adams eventually became one of the founding fathers of the United States. He helped lead the colonies as they battled for independence from Great Britain. After the formation of the United States and the new country's victory in the Revolutionary War, Adams was elected the nation's second president.

Before these accomplishments, Adams worked as a lawyer in Boston. Even though he was personally opposed to the British government, he agreed to defend Captain Thomas Preston out of a sense that it was the right thing to do. This drew the anger of many Bostonians, but Adams was soon forgiven as he led the country toward freedom.

With Liberty and Justice for All

The trial of Corporal William Wemms and the seven soldiers of

The Sons of Liberty encouraged continued protest against the British soldiers.

the 29th Regiment was set for November 27. The defense attorneys met with great difficulty in securing a fair trial for the eight accused men. The Sons of Liberty and Paul Revere's popular engraving kept the awful events of March 5 in the public eye. The lawyers knew that

A FIRSTHAND LOOK AT
PAUL REVERE'S DIAGRAM

In addition to his famous engraving, Revere also created a much less well-known, but more historically accurate, sketch of the site of the Boston Massacre, which could be used as evidence in the trials of the eight British soldiers. See page 60 for a link to read more about the sketch online.

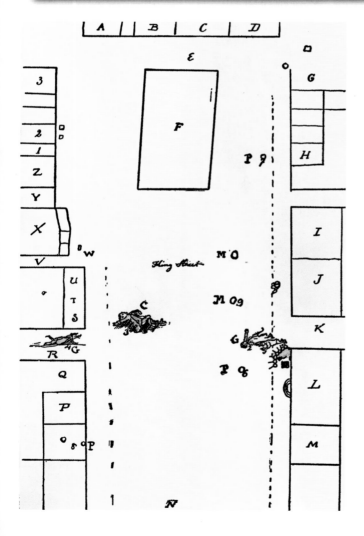

Bostonians would find the men guilty no matter what. As a result, jury selection was crucial to the outcome of the trial. When the trial opened and jurors were chosen, not one was from Boston. Instead, they came from surrounding towns. For their own safety, jurors stayed at the courthouse overnight.

Paul Revere created a diagram that was used to explain the complicated events of the Boston Massacre during the trial.

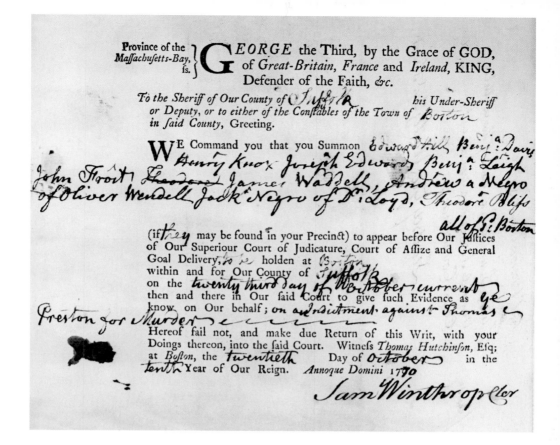

An official summons was issued to witnesses of the massacre, requiring them to testify in the trial.

Dozens of witnesses testified at the trial, and many of them had very different stories to tell. Some emphasized that the troops had provoked the citizens. One remembered that Private Matthew Kilroy had remarked in the weeks prior to the event that he would fire on the Bostonians. Four people were certain that Private Hugh White had fired. Five claimed to have seen Private Hugh Montgomery fire. Others had seen Private William Warren fire, while some accused William Wemms, John Carroll, and James Hartigan of shooting their guns. Only one witness had seen William McCauley fire.

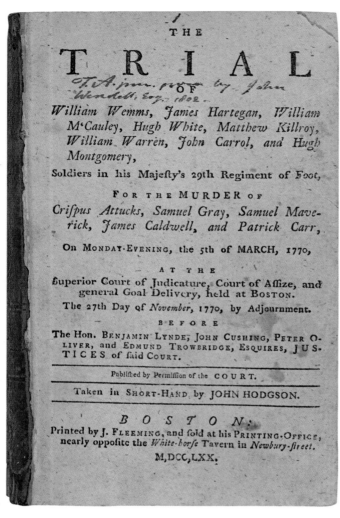

THE

TRIAL

T.A. jun. p...r... by John Wendell, Esq. 1802.

OF

William Wemms, James Hartegan, William M'Cauley, Hugh White, Matthew Killroy, William Warren, John Carrol, and Hugh Montgomery,

Soldiers in his Majesty's 29th Regiment of Foot,

FOR THE MURDER OF

Crispus Attucks, Samuel Gray, Samuel Maverick, James Caldwell, and Patrick Carr,

On MONDAY-EVENING, the 5th of MARCH, 1770,

AT THE

Superior Court of Judicature, Court of Affize, and general Goal-Delivery, held at BOSTON.

The 27th Day of *November*, 1770, by Adjournment.

BEFORE

The Hon. BENJAMIN LYNDE, JOHN CUSHING, PETER O-LIVER, and EDMUND TROWBRIDGE, ESQUIRES, JUS-TICES of faid COURT.

Publifhed by Permiffion of the COURT.

Taken in SHORT-HAND by JOHN HODGSON.

BOSTON:

Printed by J. FLEEMING, and fold at his PRINTING-OFFICE, nearly oppofite the *White-horfe* Tavern in *Newbury-ftreet.*

M,DCC,LXX.

A record of the trial was published soon afterward as a book.

Next, the defense called its witnesses. They painted a vivid picture of wild mobs attacking and insulting troops. Numerous witnesses remembered people picking up chunks of coal to throw at Private White. Bricklayer William Parker said he saw a group of young men ripping apart Faneuil Hall's butchers' stalls to make clubs. A slave named Andrew recalled a crazed Crispus Attucks knocking the musket from Kilroy's hands and screaming, "Kill the dogs, knock them over!" Andrew heard a gunshot and then, "Fire!"

The defense was masterful. By placing so much blame on Attucks, it removed most of the blame from the soldiers. It also shifted the blame away from other Boston citizens who had been present at the massacre. In closing, John Adams argued that the men should be found guilty of nothing more than **manslaughter**. In an astonishing outcome, Montgomery and Kilroy were found guilty of manslaughter. The other six were acquitted. All of the other soldiers were freed. They rejoined their regiment, which had moved on to New Jersey. When the court heard testimony against the civilian defendants on December 12, jurors quickly acquitted all four men. The trials were over.

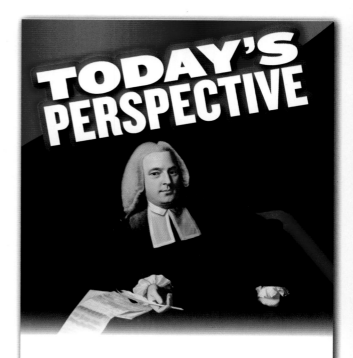

TODAY'S PERSPECTIVE

Because of the unrest in Boston following the massacre, attorneys John Adams and Samuel Quincy (above) were concerned that it would be impossible for the British soldiers to get a fair trial. However, all of the men tried were eventually freed.

Many of Boston's citizens were unhappy with Adams and Quincy for defending the soldiers. They wanted someone to pay for the March 5 killings. Today, the right to a fair trial is a major part of the U.S. justice system. Those accused of crimes are considered innocent until they are proven guilty at trial.

What Happened Where?

Boston Common

Boston Common
In 1888, a monument dedicated to Crispus Attucks was erected on Boston Common.

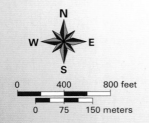

0   400   800 feet

0   75   150 meters

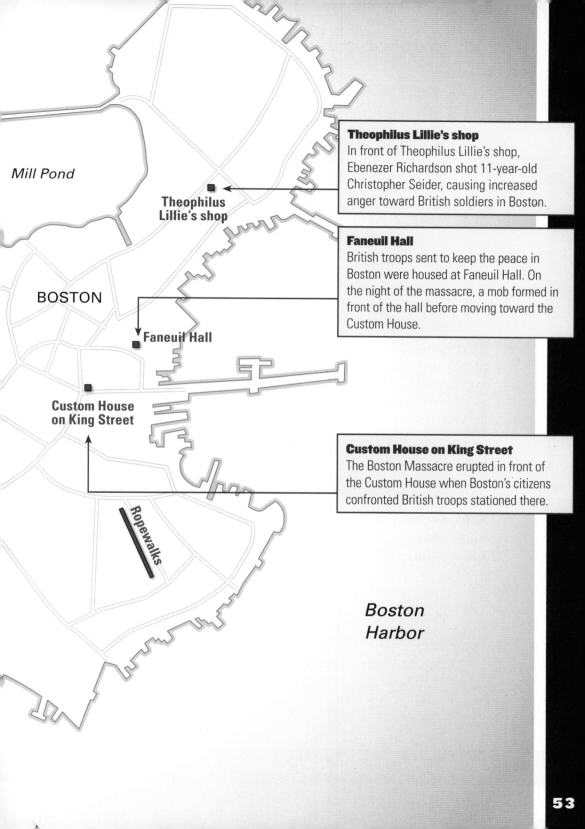

Mill Pond

Theophilus Lillie's shop

BOSTON

Faneuil Hall

Custom House on King Street

Ropewalks

Boston Harbor

Theophilus Lillie's shop
In front of Theophilus Lillie's shop, Ebenezer Richardson shot 11-year-old Christopher Seider, causing increased anger toward British soldiers in Boston.

Faneuil Hall
British troops sent to keep the peace in Boston were housed at Faneuil Hall. On the night of the massacre, a mob formed in front of the hall before moving toward the Custom House.

Custom House on King Street
The Boston Massacre erupted in front of the Custom House when Boston's citizens confronted British troops stationed there.

A New Nation

Fifty-six colonial representatives signed the Declaration of Independence, announcing the colonies' independence from Great Britain.

The trials were over, but the massacre was not forgotten. On March 5, 1771, the first anniversary of the massacre, all the bells in Boston tolled. In an April 2 speech in remembrance of the massacre, revolutionary leader James Lovell urged an overflow crowd at the Old South Meeting House to fight for liberty from the British

ROUGHLY 400,000 AMERICANS

government. Governor Hutchinson alerted Parliament about the speech, but his warning went ignored.

Just four years later, the American colonists began waging war against Great Britain. On July 4, 1776, leaders from the 13 colonies issued the Declaration of Independence, claiming themselves free from British rule. Throughout the Revolutionary War, the Boston Massacre was remembered as a reason to fight against British leadership. Today, we remember the events of March 5, 1770, as a defining moment in the formation of the United States.

The surrender of British general Charles Cornwallis in 1781 marked the end of the Revolutionary War.

FOUGHT IN THE REVOLUTIONARY WAR.

INFLUENTIAL INDIVIDUALS

Thomas Hutchinson

Paul Revere

Thomas Hutchinson (1711–1780) was acting governor of Massachusetts during the Boston Massacre.

Thomas Preston (ca. 1722– ca. 1798) was a member of the 29th Regiment of the British army. He was serving as captain of the watch on the night of the Boston Massacre.

Samuel Adams (1722–1803) was a driving force in the Loyal Nine and the Sons of Liberty. He helped lead colonists in opposing the actions of the British government.

Crispus Attucks (ca. 1723–1770) was the first victim of the Boston Massacre. Little else is known about his life.

Paul Revere (1735–1818) was a patriot and silversmith who created a popular engraving of the Boston Massacre that helped sway public opinion against the British soldiers. He is famed for his "midnight ride" on the eve of the Revolutionary War.

John Adams (1735–1826) served as the main defense attorney in the trial of the soldiers of the 29th Regiment. He later became the second president of the United States.

John Adams

Christopher Seider (1759–1770) was an 11-year-old boy who was killed by Ebenezer Richardson. Seider's death sharply escalated negative feelings toward British soldiers in Boston.

Ebenezer Richardson (?–?) was a customs informant and boycott violator. He shot and killed 11-year-old Christopher Seider after being attacked by a mob of boys.

TIMELINE

1770

February 22
Ebenezer Richardson kills Christopher Seider.

February 26
Christopher Seider's funeral draws thousands of attendants.

March 5
The Boston Massacre occurs.

1770

March 8
A funeral is held for the massacre victims.

March 10–11
The British soldiers are dispatched from Boston to Castle William.

April 21
Richardson is found guilty of murdering Seider.

October 30
The trial of Captain Thomas Preston ends in acquittal.

November 27–December 5
Eight soldiers are tried; six are acquitted and two are found guilty of manslaughter.

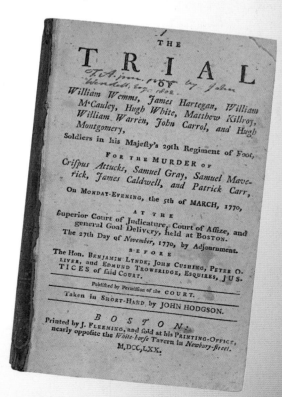

LIVING HISTORY

Primary sources provide firsthand evidence about a topic. Witnesses to a historical event create primary sources. They include autobiographies, newspaper reports of the time, oral histories, photographs, and memoirs. A secondary source analyzes primary sources and is one step or more removed from the event. Secondary sources include textbooks, encyclopedias, and commentaries. To view the following primary and secondary sources, go to www.factsfornow.scholastic.com. Enter the keywords **Boston Massacre** and look for the Living History logo Σ!.

Σ! **A Boston Massacre Obituary** A week after the Boston Massacre, the *Boston Gazette* published an obituary for the four people who died in the attack. Patrick Carr was not included in the obituary, as he had not yet died. A scan of the original obituary is available online.

Σ! **The Massachusetts Circular Letter** Samuel Adams's influential Massachusetts Circular Letter argued that the Townshend Acts were unfair because colonists had no representatives in Parliament. The letter inspired anger from Parliament and widespread support from the colonists.

Σ! **Paul Revere's Boston Massacre Engraving** Based on a drawing by Henry Pelham, Paul Revere's engraving of the Boston Massacre makes the British soldiers seem guiltier than they actually were. The engraving was seen throughout Boston and caused widespread anger against the troops. It is one of the most famous images of the Revolutionary War era.

Σ! **Paul Revere's Diagram** Prior to the trial of the eight British soldiers, Paul Revere created a historically accurate sketch of the Boston Massacre site to be used as evidence in the courtroom. A scan of the diagram, along with a detailed description, is available online.

RESOURCES

Books

Decker, Timothy. *For Liberty: The Story of the Boston Massacre.* Honesdale, PA: Calkins Creek, 2009.

Gregory, Josh. *The Revolutionary War.* New York: Children's Press, 2011.

Jeffrey, Gary. *John Adams and the Boston Massacre.* New York: Gareth Stevens, 2011.

Visit this Scholastic Web site for more information on the Boston Massacre: www.factsfornow.scholastic.com Enter the keywords Boston Massacre

GLOSSARY

acquittal (uh-KWIH-tuhl) a situation in which someone is found not guilty of a crime

autopsy (AW-tahp-see) an examination performed on a dead person to find the cause of death

boycotted (BOI-kaht-id) refused to buy something or do business with someone as a punishment or protest

colonies (KAH-luh-neez) areas settled by people from another country and controlled by that country

customs (KUHS-tuhmz) authorities responsible for regulating the goods coming into and going out of a country

economy (i-KAHN-uh-mee) the system of buying, selling, making things, and managing money in a place

export (EK-sport) send products to another country to sell them there

frontier (fruhn-TEER) the far edge of a country where few people live

imports (IM-ports) goods brought in from a foreign country

indicted (in-DITE-id) officially charged with a crime

legislatures (LEJ-uh-slay-churz) the parts of government that are responsible for making and changing laws

manslaughter (MAN-slaw-tur) the crime of killing someone without intending to do it

pardon (PARD-uhn) forgiveness of a crime

Parliament (PAR-luh-muhnt) the part of the British government that makes laws

regiments (REJ-uh-muhnts) military units made up of two or more battalions